TREES ARE KIND

with
Sherman the Squirrel
and friends

Words by
Michael Garry

Illustrations by Deborah Luken
Typography by GoodLukenDesign

*For
Aunt May*

Each and every
living tree

Has a

PERSONALTY.

7

TREES ARE
HONEST
all the time

Never lied or
stole a dime.

9

TREES ARE
LOYAL
to their core

Maple, spruce
or sycamore.

TREES SHOW
PATIENCE
as they grow

Though their birth
was long ago.

13

TREES ARE
STEADY,
firmly rooted

Trunk and branches
so well-suited.

TREES ARE
HAPPY
making leaves

Sometimes fruit
to grab with ease.

TREES ARE
ALWAYS KIND
to birds

Inviting them
without a word.

TREES REACH
OUT
to everyone

Shading us from
summer sun.

TREES ARE
FUN
to climb upon

High above
the garden lawn.

Because trees
LOVE THE EARTH
a lot

They keep it from
getting WAY TOO
HOT.

TREES HAVE COURAGE in a storm

Though the wind and rain may swarm.

But trees are
like us, after all

Despite their best
THEY
SOMETIMES
FALL.

Mostly trees are
STRONG
AND TRUE

Let's respect them,
me & you !